CONVERGE
Bible Studies

SHARING THE GOSPEL

Bible Studies

SHARING THE GOSPEL

CURTIS ZACKERY

Abingdon Press

Nashville

SHARING THE GOSPEL
CONVERGE BIBLE STUDIES

By Curtis Zackery

Library of Congress Cataloging-in-Publication Data has been requested.

ISBN: 978-1-4267-7156-9

Series Editor: Shane Raynor

13 14 15 16 17 18 19 20 21 22—10 9 8 7 6 5 4 3 2 1

Manufactured in the United States of America

CONTENTS

ABOUT THE SERIES

Converge is a new series of topical Bible studies based on the Common English Bible translation. Each title in the *Converge* series consists of four studies based around a common topic or theme. *Converge* brings together a unique group of writers from different backgrounds, traditions, and age groups.

HOW TO USE THESE STUDIES

Converge Bible studies can be used by small groups, classes, or individuals. Each study uses a simple format. For the convenience of the reader, the primary Scripture passages are included. In Insight and Ideas, the author of the study guide explores each Scripture passage, going deeper into the text and helping readers understand how the Scripture connects with the theme of the study. Questions are designed to encourage both personal reflection and group conversation. Some questions may not have simple answers. That's part of what makes studying the Bible so exciting.

Although Bible passages are included with each session, study participants may find it useful to have personal Bibles on hand for referencing other Scriptures. Converge studies are designed for use with the Common English Bible; but they work well with any modern, reliable translation.

ONLINE EXTRAS

Converge studies are available in both print and digital formats. Each title in the series has additional components that are available online, including companion articles, blog posts, extra questions, sermon ideas, and podcasts.

To access the companion materials, visit

http://www.MinistryMatters.com/Converge

Thanks for using *Converge*!

INTRODUCTION

The other day, I was on a flight headed to Miami; and as I chatted with the gentleman seated next to me, he shared that it was his first time flying. Having flown quite a few times, I immediately asked him whether he'd like to take my window seat. He had to experience his first flight with the ability to see out the window, right? Looking down at the clouds and seeing your first takeoff and landing are amazing experiences.

The flight attendant proceeded to give the preflight safety briefing, and this guy was locked in to every word. It was interesting to observe someone actually taking in all of the instructions for what to do in case of an in-flight emergency. The same information that was so intriguing and important to this new traveler had become mundane and unimportant background noise to me because I had traveled so often.

I began to listen to the flight attendant with fresh ears, reminding myself what I would need to do in the event of an actual emergency. I watched my flying companion's face and saw the concern as he realized the possibilities of what could happen during the flight. This information was important to him. It really mattered. This man had a heightened sensitivity to the fact that what happened on this airplane was literally a matter of life and death.

Once we took off, he couldn't believe it. He just wouldn't stop staring out the window, and he was smiling throughout the entire flight. It was extremely powerful to witness. His marveling at what he was seeing caused me to see things through his eyes. I considered how remarkable it is that we are able to fly.

When we started to experience turbulence for the first time, I could see how disturbing it was to him. I was able to explain that this was simply something that was a part of flying from time to time. There would be bumps that seemed as if danger was ahead, but I assured him that we would make it through OK.

The experience I had on that flight reminded me of how some followers of Jesus view the message of the gospel. The good news of salvation is information that was important to us at the beginning of our Christian journey but has since become background noise that we don't pay much attention to. We needed to know the gospel as an "entry point," but now it doesn't seem to matter as much for our everyday lives. Because we've stopped paying attention to the gospel, we forget how vitally important it is, not only for first-time hearers but for us as well.

We need to be reawakened to the glory of the gospel message, because it introduces nonbelievers to the hope of salvation *and* assures followers of Jesus through the "turbulence" we experience in life.

As we try to understand how to share the gospel, we must remember that it's not about a method; it's about a message. J.I. Packer, a great theologian, once wrote that sharing the gospel is an "endeavor to elicit a response to the truth taught. . . . It is a matter, not merely of informing, but also of inviting." We are engaging in a conversation that stems from our own life-changing experience. This is not a volume that provides a comprehensive, foolproof way to share the gospel. It's simply an encouragement toward the obedience to and fulfillment of the great commission that Jesus shared with his disciples.

In 1 Corinthians 15, Paul reminds us that the message of the gospel is of first importance. Before any other aspect of the Christian life, we must understand the significance of understanding and sharing the gospel. Paul also tells us in Romans 1:16 that the gospel is "God's own power for salvation to all who have faith in God." Let's remember the power of the gospel for the glory of God.

Let's share the gospel!

WHAT IS EVANGELISM?
SHARING THE MESSAGE OF CHRIST

SCRIPTURE
ROMANS 10:5-21

[5]Moses writes about the righteousness that comes from the Law: *The person who does these things will live by them.*[a] [6]But the righteousness that comes from faith talks like this: *Don't say in your heart, "Who will go up into heaven?"*[b] (that is, to bring Christ down) [7]or *"Who will go down into the region below?"*[c] (that is, to bring Christ up from the dead). [8]But what does it say? *The word is near you, in your mouth and in your heart*[d] (that is, the message of faith that we preach). [9]Because if you confess with your mouth "Jesus is Lord" and in your heart you have faith that God raised him from the dead, you will be saved. [10]Trusting with the heart

a Leviticus 18:5
b Deuteronomy 9:4
c Deuteronomy 30:13
d Deuteronomy 30:14

leads to righteousness, and confessing with the mouth leads to salvation. [11]The scripture says, *All who have faith in him won't be put to shame.*[e] [12]There is no distinction between Jew and Greek, because the same Lord is Lord of all, who gives richly to all who call on him. [13]*All who call on the Lord's name will be saved.*[f]

[14]So how can they call on someone they don't have faith in? And how can they have faith in someone they haven't heard of? And how can they hear without a preacher? [15]And how can they preach unless they are sent? As it is written, *How beautiful are the feet of those who announce the good news.*[g]

[16]But everyone hasn't obeyed the good news. As Isaiah says, *Lord, who has had faith in our message?*[h] [17]So, faith comes from listening, but it's listening by means of Christ's message. [18]But I ask you, didn't they hear it? Definitely! *Their voice has gone out into the entire earth, and their message has gone out to the corners of the inhabited world.*[i] [19]But I ask you again, didn't Israel understand? First, Moses says, *I will make you jealous of those who aren't a people, of a people without understanding.*[j] [20]And Isaiah even dares to say, *I was found by those who didn't look for me; I revealed myself to those who didn't ask for me.*[k] [21]But

---

e Isaiah 28:16
f Joel 2:32
g Isaiah 52:7; Nahum 1:15
h Isaiah 53:1
i Psalm 19:4
j Deuteronomy 32:21
k Isaiah 65:1

he says about Israel, *All day long I stretched out my hands to a disobedient and contrary people.*[1]

INSIGHT AND IDEAS

A few years back, before the iPhone hit the scene, I was looking for the most efficient way to text, e-mail, and surf the Web while I was traveling. I discovered the T-Mobile Sidekick. (That may reveal how far "back" those few years were.) The Sidekick offered a great user experience, and the company offered an amazing deal for unlimited use; so I knew that my budget-conscious friends would be very interested in what the phone had to offer. I began telling everyone I knew about how great the Sidekick was and all of the benefits of purchasing one. Most of the people I talked to had no idea that this phone even existed before I told them about it; but once they realized all that it had to offer, it sold itself. The carrier offered a $50 credit for every referral to purchase one, so referring 8 people kept me from having to pay my bill for a while.

WHAT IS AN EVANGELIST?

Whether I realized it or not, I had become an "evangelist" for T-Mobile. I was sharing a message that was bringing an awareness of something that many people didn't know about and vouching for the benefits of connecting with it. This story illustrates an important truth: We regularly become evangelists for what we believe in strongly.

---

1 Isaiah 65:2

The Bible says a lot about the idea of becoming an evangelist as it relates to our faith. But what does this look like? When it comes to a term like *evangelism*, it may be helpful to establish a common definition before we journey too far into this study.

A common definition of *evangelism* is "the spreading of the Christian gospel by preaching or personal witness." To become an evangelist, we have to be moved by an idea to such a degree that we feel we *must* tell others. For followers of Jesus, this idea is clearly identified as the gospel message. The important question we need to answer before we move forward is simple—what is the gospel?

WHAT IS THE GOSPEL?

Dictionary.com defines *gospel* as "the teachings of Jesus and the apostles; the Christian revelation." In the Christian church at large, we understand the word to simply mean "good news." But why is the gospel message, as it pertains to the Christian faith, good news?

Scripture tells us that everyone has sinned (Romans 3:23) and that "the wages that sin pays are death"(Romans 6:23). When humans sin, they turn away from the God who created them. The God of the universe took on flesh and lived among us in the person of Jesus Christ (John 1:14). He was crucified and died a real death for crimes he didn't commit. He was buried in and rose from a real tomb. He defeated death and is alive. As a result, we can be reconciled to this perfect and holy God (2 Corinthians 5:21).

The "good news" is that salvation, restoration, and new life are available to us, not because of our ability to be good people, but because of God's grace and love and God's desire to be in relationship with us. The most important aspect of the gospel is that *God* is the one who loves us, who saves us, who restores us, and who gives us life through Jesus Christ.

Without our understanding and acceptance of the gospel message, we cannot truly give ourselves over to Christ. When we meet Christ as Lord, we're fully aware of the impact of the gospel message in our lives. Meeting Jesus doesn't automatically make us a master theologian or a Bible scholar, but we're fully cognizant of the truth that we have been saved by grace. If we know Jesus, we have a message to share. The message of the gospel is the linchpin to evangelism. Our hope is to grow in our passion and ability to share this "good news."

IS EVANGELISM OPTIONAL?

For a long time, I was under the impression that sharing this message was only for certain Christians. I thought that specific individuals were gifted with the ability to communicate with words and that the rest of us were simply obligated to pray and hope for the best. I've even heard some believers talk about how they've invested in others so that *those* Christians could share the gospel and they wouldn't have to share it themselves. For most of my early church experience, evangelism was treated as an extra-credit-type of activity for followers of Jesus. Participating in evangelism reflected an

17

attitude of going above and beyond in our pursuit of him. Sadly, I think that many of us share this same experience in our Christian lives.

Is evangelism optional for the follower of Jesus Christ? Considering the weight of the message of the gospel, it's vital that we have an understanding of what the Bible says about the subject. Let's take a look at a few Scriptures and make our determination.

In Mark 16:15, Jesus commands his disciples to "go into the whole world and proclaim the good news to every creature." This is the final command that Jesus makes to his followers before he ascends into heaven. This fact alone makes it seem like it must be pretty important.

In Matthew 28:18-20, Jesus tells his followers, "I've received all authority in heaven and on earth." Directly after this reminder of his power to make any command, he displays that authority to them by instructing them to "go and make disciples of all nations." Through this, he's instructing them to call individuals to commit to following Jesus.

The most vivid example of the necessity of our participation in evangelism on earth comes from Romans 10:14-15, which reads, "How can they call on someone they don't have faith in? And how can they have faith in someone they haven't heard of? And how can they hear without a preacher? And how can they preach unless they are sent? As it is written, *"How beautiful are the feet of those who announce the good news."* Although it is clear throughout Scripture that the Lord has the power to draw people and still deems it necessary that we are proactive in the process of evangelism. We have to go forth. In verse 15, we see a clear encouragement for those who preach the gospel. Sharing the gospel is not only commanded, it's celebrated.

WE CAN'T FORGET THE GOSPEL

Have you ever had a set of keys, and on that key ring there's one key that you're not quite sure what it goes to? You know that it must unlock something important, but you're not quite sure what it is. You look at the key and think to yourself that it was important enough to hang on to, so it must have been significant at some point in time.

For many of us, this is how we view the gospel. We believe that it was a key that unlocked the gateway to eternal life and a connection to salvation through Jesus Christ. We even share this key with others—at first—often near the time when we initially use it ourselves. But over time, the gospel is shared less, to the point that it becomes that key that we know is important to the Christian life but can't remember what it goes to. What we must realize is that we need the gospel every day, even as followers of Jesus.

As we share the good news with others, we also preach the gospel to ourselves. We understand that the message of the gospel introduces lost and hopeless people to the hope of life through Jesus. But disciples of Jesus need to be continually reminded of the gospel message too. As we remember the despair that we were delivered from because

19

of the person and work of Jesus, we experience heartfelt joy and a sense of motivation to share the hope of rescue with others.

GOSPEL CONVERSATIONS

If the whole point of church is Jesus, then there has to be an aim in our hearts to have gospel conversations. We need to know that we are in these conversations every day. Each interaction with someone else is an opportunity for us to center our focus on the good news. Whether at school, at work, online, or on vacation, our focus should be on the promotion and exaltation of the gospel of Jesus Christ. When we begin to have this wide view of what it means to be in gospel conversations, it becomes a continual reminder of our purpose here on earth: to bring God glory and to communicate Christ's love through our actions and attitudes.

THE DRIVE IS ALREADY THERE

When we meet Jesus and truly understand that the gospel message is the most important idea that can be communicated by anyone, we shouldn't have to be motivated to go. But the reality of our situation is this: even though we are followers of Jesus, our flesh and the Spirit are at war (Galatians 5:16-17). We can actually suppress the truth and grieve the Holy Spirit. But after true introspection and prayerful consideration, we should eventually come to the understanding that no earthly pursuit or person's opinion of us can supersede the importance of the message of the gospel.

The only way that we will be outwardly focused is if we're motivated to see change happen. This motivation comes when we understand that we're the ones responsible for delivering the message that there *is* hope for us, despite the fact that sin separates us from God. This excites us about sharing.

UNDERSTANDING WHY

Why is it important for us to know why we should share the gospel? Why is it important for us to study Scripture and seek to effectively communicate God's truth to others? Because we need to feel the weight of the implications of the message that we're communicating to others. We have to come to terms with the fact that when we're in a gospel conversation with someone else, we're setting the table for a life-changing event. There will come a point in the conversation when the next thing that we say to this individual can affect his or her view of God forever.

That's pretty heavy stuff.

Of course, individuals will wrestle with the truth of the gospel for themselves. But that being said, if we're ill-prepared or we're sharing things that aren't biblically sound or are founded in our emotions rather than in the truth of what it means to connect to the gospel, we can lead others astray.

WE HAVE TO BE WILLING TO BE UNCOMFORTABLE

As we examine what it means for us to share the gospel of Christ, we will often struggle with the desire to fulfill our own selfish motivations (what some Bible translations call *the flesh*). The Bible is very clear about the fact that this will occur (Galatians 5:16-17). Our own comfort and our lack of desire to disrupt it can be barriers to effectively submitting to our responsibility to share the good news. We have to tell ourselves that it's not about us. We see throughout Scripture reminders that this life we live on earth is designed to be lived for God's glory and not our own.

What we perceive to be uncomfortable, when we're in line with the biblical mandate to share the gospel, may simply be our flesh attempting to suppress the Spirit. Evangelism is not usually the comfortable thing to do. But there are few things on earth more satisfying than leading someone else to Christ.

QUESTIONS

1. What are two kinds of righteousness, according to Paul (Romans 10:5-6)? Which one is better? Why?

2. Why is confessing Christ with our mouth so important (Romans 10:9)?

3. What is the significance of having faith in our hearts (Romans 10:9)? Is there any other kind of faith?

4. Romans 10:14 stresses the importance of preaching. Why is it important? Is it as effective now as it was in Paul's day? What are the different ways people preach now?

5. How does faith come (Romans 10:17)? Why, do you think, is this the case? Is this the only way to get faith?

6. How is God found by people who aren't looking for God today (Romans 10:20)?

7. How would you define the gospel of Christ in one or two sentences?

8. Name some things people are evangelists for today. Why is sharing the good news of Jesus Christ sometimes more difficult than sharing other kinds of "good news" to the people around us?

9. What are gospel conversations? What are some practical steps you can take that will enable you to have more of them?

10. Why does evangelism often make people so uncomfortable? What are some things that can be done to change that?

2

HOW DO I DO IT?
UNDERSTANDING SPIRIT-LED EVANGELISM

SCRIPTURE
MATTHEW 28:16-20; COLOSSIANS 4:2-6, 1 PETER 3:8-17

MATTHEW 28:16-20

[16]Now the eleven disciples went to Galilee, to the mountain where Jesus told them to go. [17]When they saw him, they worshipped him, but some doubted. [18]Jesus came near and spoke to them, "I've received all authority in heaven and on earth. [19]Therefore, go and make disciples of all nations, baptizing them in the name of the Father and of the Son and of the Holy Spirit, [20]teaching them to obey everything that I've commanded you. Look, I myself will be with you every day until the end of this present age."

COLOSSIANS 4:2-6

[2]Keep on praying and guard your prayers with thanksgiving. [3]At the same time, pray for us also. Pray that God would open a door

for the word so we can preach the secret plan[a] of Christ—which is why I'm in chains. [4]Pray that I might be able to make it as clear as I ought to when I preach. [5]Act wisely toward outsiders, making the most of the opportunity. [6]Your speech should always be gracious and sprinkled with insight so that you may know how to respond to every person.

1 PETER 3:8-17

[8]Finally, all of you be of one mind, sympathetic, lovers of your fellow believers, compassionate, and modest in your opinion of yourselves. [9]Don't pay back evil for evil or insult for insult. Instead, give blessing in return. You were called to do this so that you might inherit a blessing. [10]For

> those who want to love life
>> and see good days
> should keep their tongue from evil speaking
>> and their lips from speaking lies.
> [11]They should shun evil and do good;
>> seek peace and chase after it.
> [12]The Lord's eyes are on the righteous
>> and his ears are open to their prayers.
> But the Lord cannot tolerate
>> those who do evil.[b]

---

a or *mystery*
b Psalm 34:12-16:

[13]Who will harm you if you are zealous for good? [14]But happy are you, even if you suffer because of righteousness! Don't be terrified or upset by them. [15]Instead, regard Christ as holy in your hearts. Whenever anyone asks you to speak of your hope, be ready to defend it. [16]Yet do this with respectful humility, maintaining a good conscience. Act in this way so that those who malign your good lifestyle in Christ may be ashamed when they slander you. [17]It is better to suffer for doing good (if this could possibly be God's will) than for doing evil.

INSIGHT AND IDEAS

Many followers of Jesus will connect to the truth that we are called by God to share the message of the gospel with others. The reality, though, is that for most this truth is overwhelming. Many wonder, "How do I begin?" or "Can I even do this?" These are important questions whose answers will provide a point of connection to the mission God has set before us.

THE COWARDLY LION

When dealing with evangelism, we as believers can act a lot like a timeless character from American cinema: the Cowardly Lion in *The Wizard of Oz*. He is on a quest to find the one thing that will enhance his life: *courage*.

Throughout the film, the Cowardly Lion is afraid of things that he has absolutely no reason to be afraid of. His fears are based on the assumptions he has had and the false ideas he has leaned on in his previous life experiences.

Ultimately, the lion comes to realize that he has had the power of courage all along. He simply had to realize it and walk in it. I think you can see the parallel I'm drawing here.

So many of our perceptions about what it takes to step out in evangelism are based upon false ideas of what it will actually be like. We're often afraid of things that haven't even shown up yet.

"What if I'm rejected?"
"What if I don't know what to say?"
"What if I don't have the answers to their questions?"
"I'm not really a people person. Do I still have to evangelize?"

What we realize when we begin to evangelize is that, just like the Cowardly Lion, we have the courage inside of us the whole time. If we allow the Holy Spirit to guide us in our gospel conversations, we can trust that we will have what we need to be successful.

In the "Great Commission" passage of Matthew 28:19-20, when Jesus commands the disciples to go and share the gospel message, he doesn't leave them to figure it out for themselves. He tells them that he'll be with them until the end of the age. Basically, what this means is that we have nothing to fear, because the Holy Spirit will guide us where we need to go and tell us what to say.

SPIRIT-LED EVANGELISM

The power to change hearts and lives does not come from us. It's plain and simple. We have to recognize that the Holy

Spirit must lead and guide us as we seek to engage others with the gospel of Christ. Surprisingly enough, we can have false motivations when it comes to sharing the gospel. We certainly don't want to be led by our own ideas or motivations when we're engaged in evangelism. So, that begs the question, How do we know whether we are participating in Spirit-led evangelism?

In Galatians 5:22-23, we see a very thorough list of attributes that should be evident in our lives if we're connected to the Spirit of God. This is also the fruit that should be evident in our lives as we engage in evangelism. If our gospel conversations are not exhibiting these things, we should ask ourselves what our true motivations are.

Love: Our desire to share the gospel with others must be motivated by love. If we're not sharing the truth in love, we're not exhibiting the very reason that God granted us the opportunity for life through Jesus (John 3:16).

Joy: As we share the gospel, joy should be fully present in our hearts as a result of the understanding that we, ourselves, have been redeemed and have the opportunity to share this same truth with others.

Peace: In Christ, we have the assurance that we are rescued from sin and turned toward life. We, in our interactions, should exhibit this peace in our lives naturally.

Patience: Oftentimes when we engage in conversation over issues we're passionate about, the desire to be a good listener dissipates and we simply charge ahead with our agenda. When engaged in gospel conversations, we need to trust the power of the Holy Spirit and wait for his guidance and movement.

Kindness: Our desire is to be generous and considerate as followers of Jesus Christ. These traits should be fully evident in our conversations and interactions when it comes to evangelism.

Goodness: I've heard it said that goodness does whatever loving wisdom calls for in a given situation. This is how we want to operate as we respond in gospel conversations.

Faithfulness: Our only hope as Christians is in the power of God to do and be the things that are promised us in God's Word. This faith in which God is for us and can be for others is vital as we share the Gospel.

Gentleness: Any gospel conversation is filled with sensitive issues and questions that will affect the perceptions of God and future motivations of an individual. It is vital that we handle these moments with great care and affection.

Self-control: As human beings, our emotions have the power to get the best of us at any moment if we're not proactively seeking the guidance of the Holy Spirit. If we are engaged in a gospel conversation and this occurs, we can go a long way toward insulting others and being a poor reflection of the grace of Jesus.

The description of the fruit of the Spirit is the natural filter and grid through which we can determine our motivations and intentions for the delivery of the gospel to others. Because of the importance of evangelism in the Christian's life, we must do it completely connected to the guidance of the Spirit.

As we begin to take practical steps toward growth in our ability to engage in gospel conversations, it's imperative that we have a proper perspective on what we hope to accomplish by doing so. We're not simply attempting to convince people to adopt our religious point of view. We're delivering a message of hope that a real Savior can restore us and give us new life. The way we deliver this message is very important. This truth should cause us to continually evaluate our motives and methods.

WHAT'S OUR POWER SOURCE?

One way to explain Spirit-led gospel conversations is to compare the experience to a rushing river. A river has mighty power. We have the opportunity to build channels; and in this way, we use the force or power from the river and direct it. The channel doesn't create the power but simply allows it to flow through. When we understand that the power to preach the gospel effectively doesn't come *from* us but *through* us, we go a long way toward figuring out how to lock in to what the Lord desires for us to do in evangelism.

I remember when I was a kid, waking up on Christmas morning and rushing downstairs to see what was under the tree. The most wonderful time would be opening a present and seeing that I got the toy that I had been really wanting. Everything else would become background noise as I locked into the fact that I got the gift I'd asked for.

I remember tearing off the packaging and holding that toy in my hand and flipping the "on" switch only to realize that the batteries weren't included. Although I knew what the toy was supposed to do and I knew how it was supposed to work, it wouldn't do anything without power. This is also true for followers of Jesus. We realize the call that we have on our lives to share the message of the hope of the gospel. But without the power source, we aren't able to do what we're intended to do. That power source is the Holy Spirit.

PEOPLE AREN'T A TO-DO LIST

As Christians, sometimes we approach the command to "go and make disciples" as an item on a to-do list that must be accomplished. We know that our responsibility as followers of Christ is to share the gospel, so we set out to accomplish our work of obedience in order to make the Lord happy.

I believe that we're sadly mistaken when we take this view. Our desire to share the hope and truth of the gospel should be motivated by love and the belief that the life change that has occurred for us can happen for others. People will often detect your motivations when you're engaged in conversation with them. Many times, we approach evangelism with the wrong idea about the outcomes. This, in turn, affects the way we interact with others. Paul, in his letter to the Colossians, establishes what our conversations should look like. "Your speech should always be gracious and sprinkled with insight so that you may know how to respond to every person" (Colossians 4:6).

GRACIOUS SPEECH

When we share the gospel, we need to do so with the same heart of grace that has been extended to us by God. This will be completely evident in the way that we communicate with others. It's important to approach each conversation with kindness and humility. Evangelism shouldn't be viewed as an opportunity to argue but to share the truth of our connection with Christ and the hope of salvation for others. People may have some serious issues in their experience with God that have caused some anger and frustration. These things may manifest themselves in our dialogue with them. Responding with grace and allowing people to vent may be the very things that compel them to be open to exploring who Jesus really is. In 1 Peter 3:15, it says, "Whenever anyone asks you to speak of your hope, be ready to defend it. Yet, do this with respectful humility, maintaining a good conscience. Act in this way so that those who malign your good lifestyle in Christ may be ashamed when they slander you."

SPRINKLED WITH INSIGHT

In the English Standard Version of the Bible, this part of the verse is translated that our conversations should be "seasoned with salt." Salt is used to add flavor. This means that our conversations need to have some flavor added to them. I'm not talking about adding anything to the gospel message. But we do need to make sure that the conversation surrounding our communication is interesting and engaging. We should allow our personality to come through when we interact with others for the cause of

35

Christ. It's important for people to know that we care about this stuff.

If you're sharing with others about this amazing relationship you have with Jesus and it doesn't even seem like you're passionate about it, there's definitely a problem. You want people to be intrigued by what you're sharing with them. Share personal stories, testimonies, and insights that will display the heart behind your intentions in talking.

RESPONDING TO EVERY PERSON

Scripture tells us that we need to be prepared to "respond to every person" (Colossians 4:6). The first step toward making sure that this happens is to pay attention. We want to be fully engaged when we're in gospel conversations with others. So often, simply being a good listener creates gateways to connection. We need to make sure that we're asking questions and allowing the Holy Spirit to guide us through the encounter. In being prepared to respond, this doesn't mean that we're going to have the answers to every question that is asked of us. It also doesn't mean that we should make up answers to questions that we don't know the answer to. "I don't know" is, indeed, a response. The question is: Are we willing to journey together with that individual to address his or her questions and issues? We want to continue to rely on the truth of the gospel and simply point people to Jesus.

Our trust and reliance on the power of the Holy Spirit will provide the guidance and equipping necessary to engage in gospel conversations.

QUESTIONS

1. What is the significance of some of the disciples worshipping Jesus and others doubting (Matthew 28:17)? How is this an issue today?

2. Why does Jesus tell his followers about the authority he has been given just before he instructs them to go make disciples? What is the connection between authority and evangelism (Matthew 28:18)?

3. What is the secret plan or mystery of Christ (Colossians 4:3)?

4. How can we sprinkle our speech with insight (Colossians 4:6)? Why is this important?

5. What are some ways we can be ready to defend the hope we have in Christ?

6. What are some ways we can deal with the fear that might come when we attempt to share the gospel with others?

7. What role does the Holy Spirit play in evangelism? How can we involve the Holy Spirit more as we share Christ?

8. What do you think about scripted evangelism presentations? Have you ever used one? How effective do you think they are?

9. Why, do you think, are some people more gifted at sharing Christ than others are?

10. Why is it important to attempt to show people the intentions of our heart when we share Christ with them?

3

WHO'S THE GOSPEL FOR?
LEARNING TO REACH OUT TO EVERYONE

SCRIPTURE
MATTHEW 9:35-38; 22:34-40

MATTHEW 9:35-38

[35]Jesus traveled among all the cities and villages, teaching in their synagogues, announcing the good news of the kingdom, and healing every disease and every sickness. [36]Now when Jesus saw the crowds, he had compassion for them because they were troubled and helpless, like sheep without a shepherd. [37]Then he said to his disciples, "The size of the harvest is bigger than you can imagine, but there are few workers. [38]Therefore, plead with the Lord of the harvest to send out workers for his harvest."

MATTHEW 22:34-40

[34]When the Pharisees heard that Jesus had left the Sadducees speechless, they met together. [35]One of them, a legal expert,

tested him. [36]"Teacher, what is the greatest commandment in the Law?"

[37]He replied, *"You must love the Lord your God with all your heart, with all your being,*[a] and with all your mind. [38]This is the first and greatest commandment. [39]And the second is like it: *You must love your neighbor as you love yourself.*[b] [40]All the Law and the Prophets depend on these two commands."

INSIGHT AND IDEAS

Growing up in a bit more urban area of New Jersey, I didn't spend much time around farmland. Because New Jersey is the "garden state," there are areas where there are fields of various crops. I remember at a young age seeing the vast expanse of a healthy and thriving cornfield. I thought, *How will they be able to pick all of that corn?* There was so much delicious-looking corn that was ripe for the picking and ready to eat, but it didn't look like anyone would be getting to pick it any time soon. I asked, "How much of that corn will go to waste?" The corn was ready. All it would have taken was for someone to go and simply pick it. This is the type of imagery that the Lord is trying to get across to us in Matthew 9:37-38. There are so many who are ready to know the love of Jesus personally. All it will take is for someone to go show them and tell them.

---

a Deuteronomy 6:5
b Leviticus 19:18

THE GOSPEL IS FOR EVERYONE

Let's take another look at a Scripture that we discussed earlier. In Mark 16:15, we see the command from Jesus to the disciples to "go into the whole world and proclaim the good news to every creature." We looked at the beginning of this passage to understand that we must indeed go. Now, when attempting to understand to whom we must go, we can look to the end of the passage for our answer. What we see there is a command to take the gospel to all of creation. Matthew 28:19 reinforces the idea that we are to take the gospel to all nations. *Nations* here is translated from the Greek word *ethnos,* which means "people groups."

This premise is understandably overwhelming. As you are likely well aware, there are a *lot* of people on earth. The instruction here is a reminder that our aim as followers of Christ is that all people would hear and know of the gospel. This commission is accomplished through discipleship and continually passing down the message and command to followers of Jesus. The important thing for us to determine is what this command means for you and me.

A FEW MISSTEPS

When the power of God transformed my life, I was over-come with two very clear ideas. Number one, I was experi-encing a joy in my life that I had never thought possible until that point. Number two, I wanted to tell others around me about what I was experiencing. I immediately began to tell whoever would listen that God had changed my life and that this kind of change was available for their lives too. Although this all encompassing approach allowed me to share in quantity, it didn't allow me to approach the sharing with quality. I would simply use the same words and routine I had memorized with every individual I chatted with. Needless to say, there were many times that this scripted approach simply didn't connect with the people I was talking to. I wasn't taking the time to stop, pray, and ask the Lord what to say and to whom I should say it.

When we make sharing the gospel about following a certain process or procedure, we limit our ability to connect with the individuals whom God is calling us to connect with. The Lord may allow you to talk to a friend or peer one day and someone older or younger the next. All of these people will be in various stages of life, and that directly affects the type of conversation you'll have.

Please don't understand this as asking you to change the message that is compelling you to go. We just need to be a good steward of the opportunities that we have to share life with other individuals. We need to trust that God can speak to us and provide opportunities to talk with others about God's glory.

THE GREATEST COMMANDMENT

As with any command that we see in Scripture, our first step should always be to ask the Holy Spirit to guide us in how we are to respond properly. Too often, we take things into our own hands and think that if we're creative enough, we can simply "convince" someone to sign up for the Christian team. This should never be our goal. Our hope is to convince others that life with Christ is the best way to live.

We know that we can't count solely on our own intellect and ideas when it comes to response to the Scriptures. As we seek guidance and answers, we also know that there is a precedent set for us in Scripture for how we are to move. I once heard a man say that we should "pursue the known will of God, and the unknown will reveal itself." As we seek answers, then, we should see what the Bible lays out for us as a precedent in this matter.

In Matthew 22:36-40, Jesus was asked what the greatest commandment was. He told them that it was to "love the Lord your God with all your heart, with all your being, and with all your mind." Jesus didn't stop his answer there, however. He continued by saying "The second is like it: You must love your neighbor as you love yourself." I believe that this goes a long way toward reminding us how we should begin to respond to the question of whom we should be sharing the gospel with. We understand our need for a savior and the desire to be redeemed. We should be as burdened for our neighbor *as we are for ourselves*! What better way to love your neighbor than to share the one message of hope that has eternal ramifications?

WHO IS OUR NEIGHBOR?

Dictionary.com defines a *neighbor* as "a person who lives near another or a person or thing that is near another." We can break this down as those that are in our immediate context. As we've understood together, the Lord will lead us and guide us in where we are to go in effort to preach the gospel. One way that we can move forward in obedience in the "known will" of God is to begin with our neighbors.

The Lord may indeed be calling you to move or to travel to a distant land to share the message of the gospel. As you seek the Lord in this, it's important to understand that "all nations" includes the people who are right next door.

Honestly, for most of us, the idea of sharing the gospel in our own context is a lot more daunting than the idea of going to a foreign land with the good news. The reason for this is that there is a higher level of accountability and a greater chance of continued interaction with those with whom we share Jesus. Many times, this awakens thoughts of fear, anxiety, and inadequacy. We must dispel these thoughts immediately. Again, let us consider where the power of the gospel actually comes from. This life-changing power doesn't originate with us but with the God of the universe we're pointing people to.

UNDERSTANDING OUR NEIGHBORHOOD

In Matthew 9:37-38, we see that Jesus refers to those who haven't heard the gospel as a harvest that needs laborers to tend to it. It's extremely important for those who would properly attend to crops being harvested to know the lay of the land. The workers need to know the keys that factor into yielding a good harvest and the obstacles that might prevent a good one. In the same way, it's important for us as workers of the kingdom to understand our "harvest field," our neighborhood. Here's a list of questions that might enter into our conversation as we examine the prospect of responding to the command to preach the gospel to all nations.

What are the major issues or needs in my area?

Where are the most unchurched areas in my immediate context?

Do I know the neighbors in the houses and apartments surrounding mine?

Are there any major cultural differences—religious, ethnic, and so forth—that might be a barrier to sharing the gospel?

This isn't a comprehensive list of questions, but they can be useful as we begin to understand how to move forward in evangelism. All of these factors affect our sensitivity to our context and method of delivery in our gospel conversations. They don't change the message, but they help us stay aware of the ways that we can engage people with the good news of Christ.

WITH WHOM WILL WE SHARE THE GOOD NEWS?

We've established that the Lord is calling us, as followers, to preach the gospel to all creation. I think that the pressing question is, What does that mean for us specifically? Well let me begin to make a list: broken people, hurting people,

47

seeking people, married people, divorced people, single people, young people, old people. I think that you get my point. We truly need to be prepared to share the gospel with *all* people.

God will direct us where we need to go and to whom we need to talk with, but we can't always assume that we know exactly what type of people the Lord wants us to reach out to. You may have a specific burden for a particular people group that you want to dedicate your life to serving, but you also may be led to engage in a conversation at a coffee shop or the gas station.

There's no cookie-cutter type of interaction. We must be receptive to the Holy Spirit in every instance to lead and guide us.

POTENTIAL GOSPEL BARRIERS

As we prepare to go forward in obedience to the command that we share the gospel, it would be prudent to acknowledge the potential barriers to successfully heeding the call to go. We will talk more about preparation for our conversations, but we must first address the potential pitfalls that could keep us from sharing the gospel in the first place.

Ourselves. We can be our own biggest barrier to moving forward with the Christian message. Galatians 5:16-17 reminds us very clearly that in the life of the Christ-follower, our flesh and the Spirit of God who dwells inside of us are at war. That means that we have the potential to grieve the

Spirit and act according to the impulses and desires of our flesh. This is one way that we can be blind to the necessity for us to love our neighbor well by sharing the saving message of redemption through the gospel.

The words of others. The Bible is clear that there are people who will deliver messages that may distract us from the purpose that we are to live out as followers of Jesus. Ephesians 5:6-14 gives us a vivid example of this. If we're distracted by the belief that our own enjoyment of life and comfort is what is most important in our time on earth, we will miss the ultimate purpose that God has for us to bring God glory and direct others to God's saving grace.

Fear. In 2 Timothy 1:7-9, Paul encourages Timothy with the truth that fear doesn't come from the Lord and that he must not be ashamed of the testimony of what the Lord has done. Although we know the amazing grace and life-changing work of redemption in our own lives, at times we waver in our faith in the ability of God to do the same in others. As this verse reminds us, it is the power of God that is at work.

QUESTIONS

1. Why did Jesus heal diseases and sicknesses as he traveled from town to town (Matthew 9:35)? What role do healing and health-care ministries play in evangelism today?

2. How can we have compassion the way Jesus did in Matthew 9? Is this something we can learn to do?

3. What is the harvest Jesus refers to in Matthew 9:37? Why are there so few workers for this harvest?

4. How can the average Christian respond to Christ's call to preach the gospel to all nations (Matthew 28:19)?

5. How do we love our neighbors in the same way we love ourselves (Matthew 23:39)?

6. Who are our neighbors? Why didn't Jesus simply say that we should love everyone?

7. What is the difference between evangelism and discipleship? How do each of these accomplish the Great Commission?

8. Why is quality more important than quantity in evangelism? What are the potential pitfalls of focusing too much on numbers?

9. What are some practical steps you can take to get to know more of the people who live and work around you?

4

WHEN, WHERE, AND WHY?
FIGURING OUT WHAT TO DO NEXT

SCRIPTURE
ROMANS 1:16-17; 1 TIMOTHY 4:7-16; 2 TIMOTHY 2:22-26

ROMANS 1:16-17

[16]I'm not ashamed of the gospel: it is God's own power for salvation to all who have faith in God, to the Jew first and also to the Greek. [17]God's righteousness is being revealed in the gospel, from faithfulness[a] for faith,[b] as it is written, *The righteous person will live by faith.*[c]

1 TIMOTHY 4:7B-16

[7b]Train yourself for a holy life! [8]While physical training has some value, training in holy living is useful for everything. It has promise

---

a or *faith*
b or *faithfulness*
c Habakkuk 2:4

for this life now and the life to come. [9]This saying is reliable and deserves complete acceptance. [10]We work and struggle for this: "Our hope is set on the living God, who is the savior of all people, especially those who believe." [11]Command these things. Teach them. [12]Don't let anyone look down on you because you are young. Instead, set an example for the believers through your speech, behavior, love, faith, and by being sexually pure. [13]Until I arrive, pay attention to public reading, preaching, and teaching. [14]Don't neglect the spiritual gift in you that was given through prophecy when the elders laid hands on you. [15]Practice these things, and live by them so that your progress will be visible to all. [16]Focus on working on your own development and on what you teach. If you do this, you will save yourself and those who hear you.

2 TIMOTHY 2:22-26

[22]Run away from adolescent cravings. Instead, pursue righteousness, faith, love, and peace together with those who confess the Lord with a clean heart. [23]Avoid foolish and thoughtless discussions, since you know that they produce conflicts. [24]God's slave shouldn't be argumentative but should be kind toward all people, able to teach, patient, [25]and should correct opponents with gentleness. Perhaps God will change their mind and give them a knowledge of the truth. [26]They may come to their senses and escape from the devil's trap that holds them captive to do his will.

INSIGHT AND IDEAS

While growing up, I had a great friend who would attend an exclusive basketball camp in the summer. I was just beginning to gain an interest in basketball and getting better. We had participated in school teams and summer leagues together, but this camp was providing a more in-depth type of learning. Although he wasn't a basketball coach or a "teacher," he would show me the skills and drills that he was learning at the camp. The only thing that qualified him to teach me was that he had learned something that I didn't know. He simply taught what he had learned that day. Then he would go back to the camp and learn some more. At times, he would even stumble through trying to explain to me the things that he was trying to teach me. He was just excited about what he was learning and experiencing and wanted to share it with me so that I could experience the same positive effect on my game that he was seeing on his.

MOTIVATION

The excitement that accompanies a life-changing experience in understanding the truth of the gospel creates a motivation for us to share it with others because of the effect we know it can have on their lives. Theologian Karl Barth once said, "When it comes to the Christian life, all of us are amateurs." This is the proper encouragement for those who may feel intimidated by the idea of sharing the hope of the gospel with others. The change that we experience as a result of the gospel is what qualifies us to share it in the first place. Unfortunately, our temptation many times is to "wait until we know more" when it comes to talking about following Jesus or the truth of the Bible. Sometimes we are locked in on the idea that only pastors or people who work in churches have the ability or the right to share about these matters. Nothing could be farther from the truth. Regardless of how insecure we might feel, we should always be on the lookout for opportunities to engage in gospel conversations.

HEART CHECK

Although I'm a firm believer that once we connect to the truth of the gospel in our lives, we're prepared to share the gospel, I do feel that it is valid to examine our hearts for preparedness. There are times that we can allow ourselves to become consumed with issues that are not connected to the core of our desire to see others understand the love and grace of Jesus. In 2 Timothy 2:23-26, it says, "Avoid foolish and thoughtless discussions, since you know that they produce conflicts." We must continue to examine our hearts to make sure that our motivations are pure as we seek to share the gospel.

REMEMBER WHO THE SAVIOR IS

In the movie *The Matrix,* there is an interchange between two of the main characters, Neo and Morpheus. Neo has been exploring the idea that there is more to life as he knows it. Morpheus then presents an opportunity for

Neo to discover the "deeper truths" that he knows Neo is looking for. In their dialogue, Morpheus shares two very profound statements. One is, "Remember, I am only presenting the truth, nothing more." And the other is, "I can only *show* you the door, you have to choose to open it."

We don't make choices for other individuals. We share the joy and hope that we have found in the God of the gospel. A key verse to remember is 1 Timothy 4:16, when Paul is reminding Timothy to "Focus on working on your own development and on what you teach. If you do this, you will save yourself and those who hear you." The most relieving truth about sharing the gospel with others is that we don't have to save anyone. We're simply pointing people to life in Jesus Christ. *He* is the one who redeems lives. We, as human beings, have no power on our own to turn anyone from sin, but we can tell others about the God who does. This verse reminds us, though, that our lives and our words are used for God's glory and to lead people to God.

There is power in sharing the gospel. It's a plain and simple truth—not because of the words or methods used but because of the God that we are sharing. In Romans 1:16, Paul tells us that the gospel message is "God's own power for salvation." If we can remember that the power doesn't come from us, we'll go a long way toward connecting the heartbeat of God with those who are living a life apart from the Lord.

WHERE DO WE BEGIN?

Pray. It's the starting point for any effort to share the gospel. If we're serious about the idea of Spirit-led evangelism, then we should begin the process of sharing with listening. I know that it may seem counterintuitive,but this is the only proper way to begin to know where we should share the gospel. Our hope in evangelism rests solely on God's ability to transform people's hearts and lives. If we are going to trust God's power to change, why wouldn't we trust God's guidance to lead us to people and to conversations? We should pray that the Lord would begin to stir the hearts of those we'll meet and begin to draw them toward God's love. Because we're trusting that the Lord will guide us in our gospel conversations, we can move forward with the confidence that God will be with us as we interact with others.

Study. The Bible is the most tangible and accessible communication of God's Word and instruction for our lives. In 2 Timothy 3:16-17, it says "Every scripture is inspired by God and is useful for teaching, for showing mistakes, for correcting, and for training character, so that the person who belongs to God can be equipped to do everything that is good." If we are looking for the best way to be prepared for the interactions that the Lord will provide for us, we can find that instruction in the Scriptures. Not only will the Bible prepare us for gospel conversations, it will also offer answers for those who have questions about the message we're communicating. Although it doesn't take much to get started, we can continue to grow deeper in our knowledge and ability to communicate God's truth. As a matter of fact, it is our responsibility to be stewards of the grace that God has bestowed upon us.

PRACTICING INTENTIONALITY

Intentionality is key. It's important to know what you hope to accomplish as you set out to share the gospel. If the gospel is going to be an expression of, rather than a part of, your life, the most logical place to begin is in your regular spaces. If you're a student, you likely spend a lot of time at your place of learning. There are a lot of natural relationships that already exist for you there. The same is true for the workplace, the gym, or even family environments. You don't have to go far to find people who might be interested in exploring the truth of Jesus Christ. The message that we are sharing is one that should be having an impact on every aspect of our lives. What better places would there be to share than the ones where we spend the most time?

BE OPEN TO NEW CONVERSATIONS.

As I was growing in my faith and my desire to share that faith with others, I began asking God in prayer to show me some new ways that I could engage people in gospel conversations. I had a very simple but profound revelation—start some new conversations. (That isn't really profound at all, but it *is* simple.) If we don't interact with new people, we won't have the opportunity to share the Jesus with more people.

I spend a lot of time reading and studying at coffee shops. There's something about that environment that helps to stimulate my creativity and thinking processes. A while back, I realized that I had been spending a lot of time at the coffee shop with my earphones in, focused on the work at hand. So rather than find a table away from everyone in order to seclude myself, I began praying and asking the Lord to show me whom I could ask to join at his or her table. I cannot tell you the number of interesting and encouraging conversations that I've been blessed to participate in as a result of this simple practice. I understand that this particular opportunity of connection may be a bit intimidating to some, but there's a way that will flow with your personality and connect to your heart so that you can reach others for Christ. Find it.

IT'S NOT ALWAYS LIKE YOU PLANNED

In looking back on my early days as a Christ follower, I have to be honest and say that I'm a bit ashamed of some of the ways that I chose to share the gospel. A lot of times, I had preconceived ideas about the way I expected the conversation to go and the reality was nothing close to that. Because of this, I wasn't ready to respond properly to questions and points of view that were contrary to my position. First Peter 3:15-16 tells us, "Regard Christ as holy in your hearts. Whenever anyone asks you to speak of your hope, be ready to defend it. Yet do this with respectful humility, maintaining a good conscience." We need to be ready to respond to those who are asking us for reasons for the hope that we have. Our job is to participate in conversation that provides a safe place for these types of questions. Not every gospel conversation will end in an amazing "lightning flash" conversion story. We have to trust that we are being obedient to God's leading and that the Lord will do the work in the hearts of others.

REMEMBER THE POINT

At the end of the day, we have to be honest with ourselves about what the ultimate objective is when it comes to evangelism. For some, the opportunity to win an argument is the priority. For others, the opportunity to convince another individual to come to his or her "side" of the faith is what appeals. In talking about sharing the gospel, we can forget the bare-bones truth of what we are discussing. Jesus is the prize.

We preach so that others will have the opportunity to be turned from sin. We preach so that people might be rescued from habits, addictions, and other dangers that trip them up. We preach so that people will live with God forever. These are all true statements.

But the most important idea that compels us to preach the good news is that others will connect to Jesus. A relationship with our creator is the life-giving essence of the gospel. Jesus tells us in John 10:10, "The thief enters only to steal, kill, and destroy. I came so that they could have life—indeed, so that they could live life to the fullest." Jesus is not merely speaking of life after death. He is talking about the opportunity to experience the fullness of life on earth.

61

QUESTIONS

1. How is the gospel God's power for salvation (Romans 1:6)?

2. What does it mean to have faith in God (Romans 1:16)?

3. What does Paul mean when he says that the gospel is the power for salvation "to the Jew first and also to the Greek" (Romans 1:16)?

4. How do we train ourselves for a holy life (1 Timothy 4:7)?

5. How is holy living useful for everything (1 Timothy 4:8)?

6. Why is focusing on our own development important as we set out to share our faith in Christ?

7. What kinds of "foolish and thoughtless discussions" should we avoid as we share the gospel? How can we avoid them? Why is it important?

8. What role does teaching play in evangelism?

9. Why is prayer the best starting point for Spirit-led evangelism?

10. What are some ways you can be more intentional about sharing your faith with those around you?

11. What should be the goal for the outcome of an evangelism encounter?

CONVERGE

Bible Studies

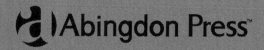

Made in the USA
San Bernardino, CA
31 August 2016